Medieval Lovers

A BOOK OF DAYS

Medieval Lovers

A BOOK OF DAYS

Poems selected by
KEVIN CROSSLEY-HOLLAND

WEIDENFELD & NICOLSON

Created and produced by PHOEBE PHILLIPS EDITIONS
Copyright this edition © Phoebe Phillips Editions 1988

Published by Weidenfeld & Nicolson, New York
A Division of Wheatland Corporation
841 Broadway, New York, New York 10003-4793

ISBN 1-55584-299-2

Designed by Rachael Foster
Origination by CLG, Verona, Italy
Printed in Portugal by
Printer Portuguesa Industria Grafica, LDA.

First Edition
10 9 8 7 6 5 4

Illustrations
Half Title: *The pursuit of love*
Title: *Aphrodite inspires a kiss*
Prologue: *The bride and groom, after the feast*

Foreword

How love fascinated men and women in medieval Europe. They sang about it; they portrayed it; and they wrote about it in poetry and prose spiritual and bawdy, thoughtful and witty, erotic and didactic.

This enchanting Day Book combines words and images to illustrate some of the medieval attitudes to love, and in particular the phenomenon known as courtly love. This convention, almost a religion, originated in the aristocratic troubadour songs of eleventh century Provence, and its articles of faith – idealisation of the beloved, unswerving devotion and suffering – influenced writers throughout medieval Europe.

Some of the brief texts are dramatic, some lyrical and some philosophical. Drawn from an exceptionally wide range of sources, they include extracts from great writers like Geoffrey Chaucer and Sir Thomas Malory in England, Marie de France and Chrétien de Troyes in France, Wolfram von Eschenbach in Germany and Dante in Italy; but they also range far afield to the fringes of Europe and beyond, with piercing lyrics from Ireland and Scotland, love-warnings from Iceland and Georgia, and a cautionary tale from Persia.

Each text has been specially or recently translated into modern English with the exception of poems by Thomas Hoccleve and William Dunbar which are printed in the original with glossaries underneath. But devotees of Robert Burns (and is there any country without them?) are unlikely to have much trouble with Mr Dunbar!

As I read the words of great poet, unpretentious epistolist and margin doodler, I am conscious of listening to voices carried over from another time. But I am also keenly aware of that far-off time brought most tantalisingly close. Here are the attitudes that underlie present-day notions about romantic love. Here are words that stir the mind and move the heart. Here are women and men not at all unlike you or me.

Kevin Crossley-Holland

Prologue

The Laws of Love

1 Thou shalt avoid avarice like the plague and shall embrace its opposite.

2 Thou shalt keep thyself chaste for the sake of her whom thou lovest.

3 Thou shalt not knowingly strive to break up another's love affair.

4 Thou shalt not choose for thy love anyone whom a natural sense of shame forbids thee to marry.

5 Be careful to avoid any kind of falsehood.

6 Do not let too many people know of your affair.

7 Being obedient in all things to the commands of ladies, you must always try to ally yourself to the service of love.

8 In giving and receiving love's solaces let modesty be ever present.

9 Thou shalt speak no evil.

10 Thou shalt not reveal love-affairs.

11 Thou shalt be in all things polite and courteous.

12 In practising the solaces of love, thou shalt not exceed the desires of thy lover.

Latin (France) · Late 12th century
Andreas Capellanus: The Art of Courtly Love

January

1

2

3

4

5

6

7

A knight offers a tiny ruby heart to his lady

Your love and my love
keep each other company —
that is why I am so joyful.
That your heart is constant
in its love for mine
is a solace beyond compare.
Yours is the clasp
that holds my loyalty,
you dismiss all my heart's sorrow.
And yours is a devotion
that does not bend or alter —
just as the Antarctic Pole
stands opposite the North Star,
and neither moves,
your love and my love
shall be steadfast in their loyalty
and never drift apart.

German · Early 13th century
Wolfram von Eschenbach: Parzival

January

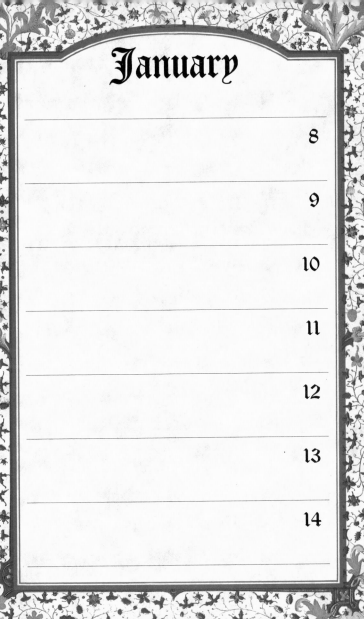

8

9

10

11

12

13

14

January

15

16

17

18

19

20

21

A queen accepts the gift of a book

I have a gentle cock,
Croweth me day:
He doth me risen erly
My matins for to say.

I have a gentle cock,
Comen he is of gret:
His comb is of red coral,
His tail is of jet.

I have a gentle cock,
Comen he is of kinde:
His comb is of red coral,
His tail is of inde.

His legges ben of asor,
So gentle and so smale:
His spores arn of silver whit
Into the wortewale.

His eynen arn of cristal,
Loken all in aumber:
And every night he percheth him
In mine ladye's chaumber.

English · Early 15th century · Anonymous

January

22

23

24

25

26

27

28

If you want to win a woman's love
and enjoy her favours,
make her a fair promise and then stick to it.
Nobody objects to the pleasures he gets!

Icelandic · 10th–12th century · Havamal

The triumph of love, Cupid, over the intellect

January

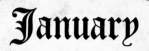

29

30

31

Love like heat and cold
    Pierces and then is gone;
Jealousy when it strikes
    Sticks in the marrowbone.

Irish · 15th–early 16th century · Anonymous

February

1

2

3

4

5

6

7

A travelling salesman tempts a pretty girl

Revered and worshipful and my most
well-beloved Valentine, I commend
myself to you with all my heart, longing
to hear all is well with you; and I beseech
Almighty God to keep you well,
according to His pleasure and your heart's
desire. And if it please you to know
how I am, I am not well in body or heart,
nor shall I be until I hear from you.

By your own M.B.
February 1477

English · Late 15th century
The Paston Letters *(Margery Brews to John Paston III)*

February

_____

8

_____

9

_____

10

_____

11

_____

12

_____

13

_____

14

_____

February

15

16

17

18

19

20

21

Lovers talking quietly in the garden

Nowadays, men cannot love for seven nights but they must have all their desires. It stands to reason this kind of love cannot last: what is soon achieved and quickly heats also quickly cools. That is how love is nowadays, soon hot soon cold: this is no stability. But the old love was not so; men and women could love each other for seven years, and no wanton lusts came between them, and that was true love, honest and faithful. And lo, love was held in the same esteem in the days of King Arthur.

English · 15th century
Sir Thomas Malory: Le Morte d'Arthur

February

_____

22

_____

23

_____

24

_____

25

_____

26

_____

27

_____

28/9

_____

March

1

2

3

4

5

6

7

Stately couples stroll arm in arm

Your eyen two will slay me suddenly;
I may the beauty of them not sustain,
So woundeth it throughout my heart keen.

And but your word will healen hastily
My heart's wound, while that it is green,
  Your eyen two will slay me suddenly;
  I may the beauty of them not sustain.

Upon my truth I say you faithfully
That you are of my life and death the queen;
For with my death the truth shall be seen.
  Your eyen two will slay me suddenly;
  I may the beauty of them not sustain,
  So woundeth it throughout my heart keen.

English · Late 14th century
Geoffrey Chaucer: Merciless Beauty

March

8

9

10

11

12

13

14

March

15

16

17

18

19

20

21

The lover and his rose

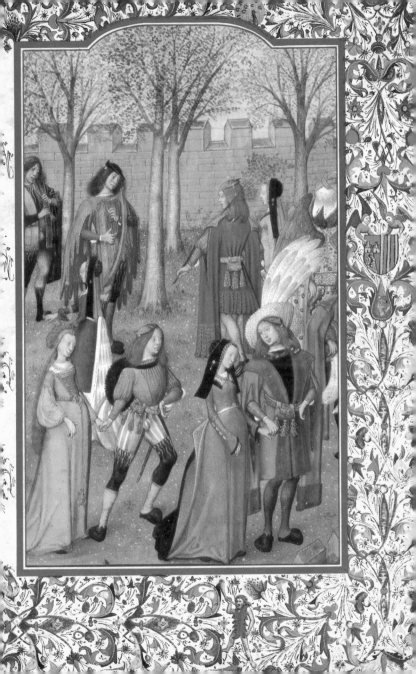

When whiting walk in forests and give deer chase,
And in the park herrings raise their horns and blow,
And flounders and moorhens in the fens embrace,
And one fish shoots another with his cross-bow,
And goslings ride out hunting to lay the wolf low,
And smelts carry spears by way of defence –
Then put in a woman your trust and confidence.

When sparrows build churches and steeples high,
And wrens carry sacks to the mill,
And curlews put clothes on clothes horses to dry,
And seagulls bring butter to market to sell,
And wood-pigeons with hunting-knives seek to kill,
And gryphons to goslings do obedience –
Then put in a woman your trust and confidence.

English · 15th century · Anonymous

March

22

23

24

25

26

27

28

J will tell you what inordinate love is:
Insanity and frenzy of mind,
Inextinguishable burning, devoid of happiness,
A great hunger that can never be satisfied,
A dulcet sickness, sweetness evil and blind,
A most wonderful sugared sweet error,
Without respite, against human nature,
It is to have vast incessant labour.

English · 15th century · Anonymous

Temptation from a hopeful lover

March

29

30

31

Love without anxiety and without fear
Is fire without flames and without warmth,
Day without sunlight, hive without honey,
Summer without flower, winter without frost.

French · Late 12th century · Chrétien de Troyes: Cligès

April

_____ 1

_____ 2

_____ 3

_____ 4

_____ 5

_____ 6

_____ 7

The Rose Garden of Love

In serenest spring you'll see
Julie by the greenwood tree
in her sister's company –
 Dulcis amor!
who pass you by when spring is nigh
 care nothing for!

Now that trees are blossoming
birds lasciviously sing,
maidens' dream are on the wing –
 Dulcis amor!
who pass you by when spring is nigh
 care nothing for!

Now that lilies bloom again
to the gods in heavenly train
girls direct their hearts' refrain –
 Dulcis amor!
who pass you by when spring is nigh
 care nothing for!

Could I clasp whom I adore
on the forest's leafy floor,
how I'd kiss her – Oh and more!
 Dulcis amor!
who pass you by when spring is nigh
 care nothing for!

Latin (Bavaria) · Late 12th–early 13th century
Anonymous: Carmina Burana

April

_____

8

_____

9

_____

10

_____

11

_____

12

_____

13

_____

14

_____

April

15

16

17

18

19

20

21

Lucrezia welcomes her secret lover

When I see the lark
moving its wings in joy
against the light
until at last it forgets
and lets itself fall
by reason of the sweetness
that fills its heart,
oh, such envy comes to me
of those whose happiness I see
that I marvel that
my heart does not melt away
at once with desire!

French · 12th century · Bernard de Ventadour

April

_____

22

_____

23

_____

24

_____

25

_____

26

_____

27

_____

28

_____

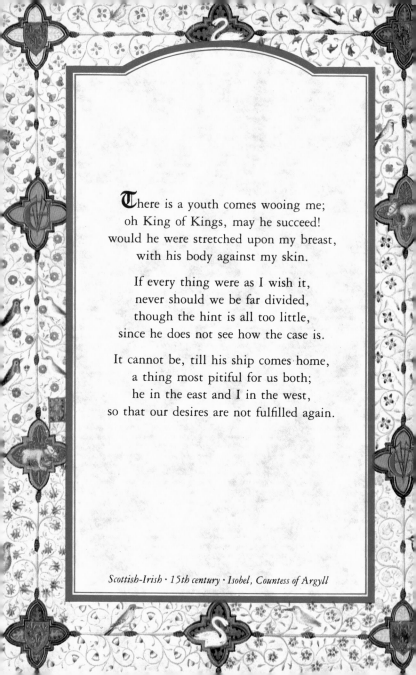

There is a youth comes wooing me;
oh King of Kings, may he succeed!
would he were stretched upon my breast,
with his body against my skin.

If every thing were as I wish it,
never should we be far divided,
though the hint is all too little,
since he does not see how the case is.

It cannot be, till his ship comes home,
a thing most pitiful for us both;
he in the east and I in the west,
so that our desires are not fulfilled again.

Scottish-Irish · 15th century · Isobel, Countess of Argyll

April

29

30

A troubadour and his lady

May

1

2

3

4

5

6

7

The first picnic of the year

Just as trees and herbs burgeon
and flourish in May, the lusty heart
that beats in every lover springs,
burgeons, buds and flourishes in
lusty deeds. For the lusty month
of May gives all lovers courage, and
constrains them to do things they
would not do in any other month.
For then all the herbs and trees
renew a man and woman, and in
like wise lovers call to mind earlier
gentleness and earlier service, and
many kind deeds forgotten
by negligence.

English · 15th century · Sir Thomas Malory: Le Morte d'Arthur

May

8

9

10

11

12

13

14

May

15

16

17

18

19

20

21

An enclosing wall for two lovers

Now is the time at hand,
Love come to blossom,
Ripens the little maid,
Swells now the tender breast.
Vainly hath all been done
    If all is ended.

Since, love, our minds are one,
    What of our doing?
Set now your arms on mine,
    Joyous our wooing.
O Flower of all the world,
    Love we in earnest!

Honey is sweet to sip
    Out of the comb.
What mean I? That will I
    Show, little one.
Not words but deeds shall be
    Love's best explaining.

Latin (Bavaria) · Late 12th–early 13th century · Anonymous

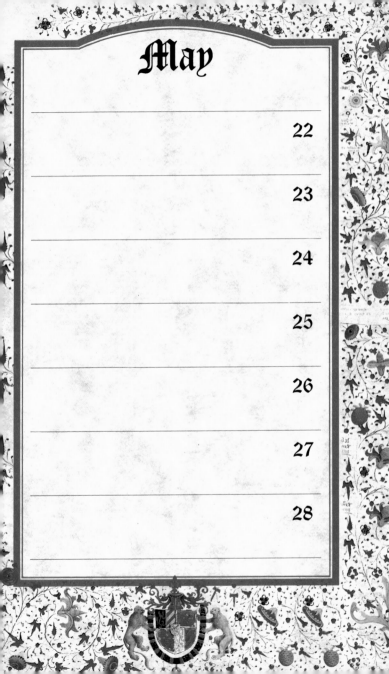

May

22

23

24

25

26

27

28

That love is suffering is easy to see, for before the love becomes equally balanced on both sides there is no torment greater, since the lover is always in fear that his love may not gain its desire and that he is wasting his efforts. . . .

If he is a poor man, he also fears that the woman may scorn his poverty; if he is ugly, he fears that she may despise his lack of beauty or may give her love to a more handsome man; if he is rich, he fears that his parsimony in the past may stand in his way. To tell the truth, no one can number the fears of one single lover.

Latin (France) · Late 12th century
Andreas Capellanus: The Art of Courtly Love

May

_____

29

_____

30

_____

31

_____

Whispering sweet words

June

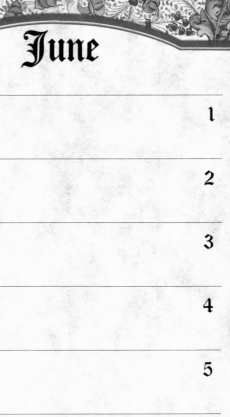

1

2

3

4

5

6

7

A bride led to her wedding feast

$\mathfrak{Y}$our mouth provokes me,
                'Kiss me, kiss sweet!'
Each time I see you so it seems to me.
But Caution stands so close it cannot be;
This is the reason for my grieving heart.
But keep your word now here alone we meet,
Give me a sweet sweet kiss or two or three!

    Your mouth provokes me,
                    'Kiss me, kiss sweet!'
    Each time I see you so it seems to me.

Caution hates me – why so I can't make out –
He wrecks my plans and tries to ruin me.
God grant that I may see him burn and die,
And live to stamp his ashes underfoot!

    Your mouth provokes me,
                    'Kiss me, kiss sweet!'
    Each time I see you so it seems to me.

English · Early 15th century · Charles d'Orleans

June

8

9

10

11

12

13

14

June

15

16

17

18

19

20

21

Seduction — the delights of temptation are clear

Take thou this rose, O Rose,
    Since Love's own flower it is,
And by that rose
    Thy lover captive is.

Smell thou this rose, O Rose,
And know thyself as sweet
As dawn is sweet.

Look on this rose, O Rose,
And looking, laugh on me,
And in thy laughter's ring
The nightingale shall sing.

Kiss thou this rose, O Rose,
That it may know the scarlet of thy mouth.

O Rose, this painted rose
    Is not the whole,
Who paints the flower
    Paints not its fragrant soul.

Latin (Bavaria) · Late 12th–early 13th century
Anonymous: Carmina Burana

June

_____ 22

_____ 23

_____ 24

_____ 25

_____ 26

_____ 27

_____ 28

A lover, tired out by the tears he wept,
Lay in exhaustion on the earth and slept;
When his beloved came and saw him there,
Sunk fast in sleep, at peace, without a care,
She took a pen and in an instant wrote,
Then fastened to his sleeve, a little note.
When he awoke and read her words his pain
(Increased a thousandfold) returned again –
'If you sell silver in the town,' he read,
'The market's opened, rouse your sleepy head;
If faith is your concern, pray through the night –
Prostrate yourself until the dawning light;
But if you are a lover, blush with shame;
Sleep is unworthy of the lover's name!
A man who sleeps before death's sleep I call
A lover of himself, and that is all!
You've no idea of love, and may your sleep
Be like your ignorance – prolonged and deep!'

Persian · 12th century
Farid ud-Din Attar: The Conference of Birds

June

_____

29

_____

30

_____

A dance of flowers

July

_____ 1

_____ 2

_____ 3

_____ 4

_____ 5

_____ 6

_____ 7

The bride-to-be displaying her ring

𝔄 rustical rosebud
    arose with the sun,
took flock and took crook
    and some wool to be spun.

Her little flock boasted
    a sheep and a she-goat,
a heifer, a bullock,
    an ass and a he-goat.

She spotted a scholar
    ensconced by a tree:
'What are you doing, sir? –
    Come and do me!'

Latin (Bavaria) · Late 12th–early 13th century
Anonymous: Carmina Burana

July

_____

8

_____

9

_____

10

_____

11

_____

12

_____

13

_____

14

_____

July

15

16

17

18

19

20

21

Lovers united under a branch of fennel

The nightingale said:
A girl may take what man she chooses
And doing so, no honour loses,
Because she did true love confer
On him who lies on top of her.
Such love as this I recommend:
To it, my songs and teaching tend.
But if a wife be weak of will –
And women are soft-hearted still –
And through some jester's crafty lies,
Some chap who begs and sadly sighs,
She once perform an act of shame,
Shall I for that be held to blame.
If women will be so unchaste,
Why should the slur on me be placed?
I cannot cease to sing my airs
Because bad wives have love affairs.

English · Late 12th–early 13th century
Anonymous: The Owl and the Nightingale

July

22

23

24

25

26

27

28

I wish her well, she wills me woe;
I am her friend, but she's my foe:
I think my heart will break in two
    With sighs and care.
With God's own greeting may she go,
    So white, so fair!

I wish I were a throstle-cock,
A bunting or a laverock,
    Sweet birds of the air!
Between her kirtle and her smock
    I'd hide, I swear.

English · Late 13th–early 14th century · Anonymous

A quiet domestic scene of contentment

July

_____

29

_____

30

_____

31

_____

Love is not honourable,
unless it is based on equality.
A poor man, if he is loyal
and possesses wisdom and merit,
is of greater worth
and his love more joyful
than that of a prince or king
who lacks loyalty.

French · Late 12th century · Marie de France: Equitan

August

1

2

3

4

5

6

7

Even out hunting there was time for love

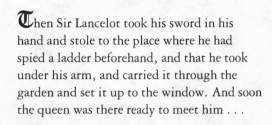

Then Sir Lancelot took his sword in his hand and stole to the place where he had spied a ladder beforehand, and that he took under his arm, and carried it through the garden and set it up to the window. And soon the queen was there ready to meet him . . .

'I wish,' said the queen, 'I wish as much as you that you might come in to me.'

'Do you wish, madam,' said Sir Lancelot, 'with your heart that I were with you?'

'Yes, truly,' said the queen.

'Then I shall prove my might,' said Sir Lancelot, 'for your love.'

And then he laid his hands on the bars of iron and pulled at them with such might that he ripped them right out of the stone walls. And one of the bars of iron cut through the flesh of his hands to the bone. And then he leaped into the chamber to the queen.

English · 15th century · Sir Thomas Malory: Le Morte d'Arthur

August

8

9

10

11

12

13

14

August

15

16

17

18

19

20

21

The Garden of Love in the warm evenings of summer

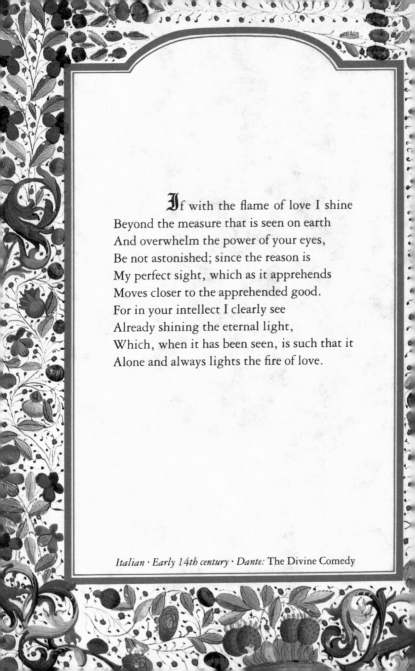

If with the flame of love I shine
Beyond the measure that is seen on earth
And overwhelm the power of your eyes,
Be not astonished; since the reason is
My perfect sight, which as it apprehends
Moves closer to the apprehended good.
For in your intellect I clearly see
Already shining the eternal light,
Which, when it has been seen, is such that it
Alone and always lights the fire of love.

Italian · Early 14th century · Dante: The Divine Comedy

August

22

23

24

25

26

27

28

She could be so blithe and gay
When so inclined, that I can say
That she was like a torch so bright
That everyone could take its light
Yet never make that light the less.

English · 14th century
Geoffrey Chaucer: The Book of the Duchess

Attendants at the Court of Love

August

29

30

31

She stood in her scarlet gown,
If anyone touched her
The gown rustled.
Eia.
She stood, her face like a rose,
Shining she stood
And her mouth was a flower.
Eia
She stood by the branch of a tree,
And writ her love on a leaf.

Latin (Bavaria) · Late 12th–early 13th century
Anonymous: Carmina Burana

September

1

2

3

4

5

6

7

Young couples encouraged by the Three Graces

I newly have a garden
Which newly is begun:
I know not such a garden
Beneath the sun.

I've a pear-tree in the middle
Of my garden there:
Mature fruit it grows not,
But early Jennet-pear.

The prettiest girl in our town
Begged a boon of me:
To graft for her a scion
From my pear-tree.

When I'd done the grafting
Entirely to her pleasure,
With wine and ale she plied me
In fullest measure.

This scion I had grafted
Right up in her home,
And twenty weeks later
It quickened in her womb.

I met that pretty maiden
After just a year:
She said it was a Robert-,
No early Jennet-pear!

English · 13th–14th century · Anonymous

September

8

9

10

11

12

13

14

September

15

16

17

18

19

20

21

The mandragora helps lovers to sleep

Euer midniges

Heart-whole, I started to beseech
That she would be my lady sweet.
I swore to her with heartfelt heat
My steadfast duty firm and true,
And love that would be always new.
To guard her honour evermore,
And serve no other, then I swore
To do my best. I promised this:
"For yours is all that ever there is,
My sweetheart. Barring dreams untrue,
I never shall be false to you,
As sure as God's intents prevail!"

'And when I thus had told my tale,
God knows, my love in pain and awe
She seemed to think not worth a straw.
To tell it briefly as it is,
Her answer was most truly this:
I cannot perfectly convey
Exactly what she had to say:
The gist of it was simply "No"
And nothing more.

English · 14th century
Geoffrey Chaucer: The Book of the Duchess

September

22

23

24

25

26

27

28

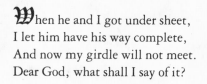

When he and I got under sheet,
I let him have his way complete,
And now my girdle will not meet.
Dear God, what shall I say of it?

Ah dear God, I am forsaken
    Now my maidenhead is taken!

English · 15th century · Anonymous

Fulfilment of desire

September

_____

29

_____

30

_____

Noble lady, I ask nothing of you
save that you should accept me
as your servant. I will serve you
as a good lord should be served,
whatever the reward may be.
Here I am, then, at your orders,
sincere and humble, gay and courteous.
You are not, after all, a bear or a lion,
and you will not kill me, surely,
if I put myself between your hands.

French · 12th century · Bernard de Ventadour

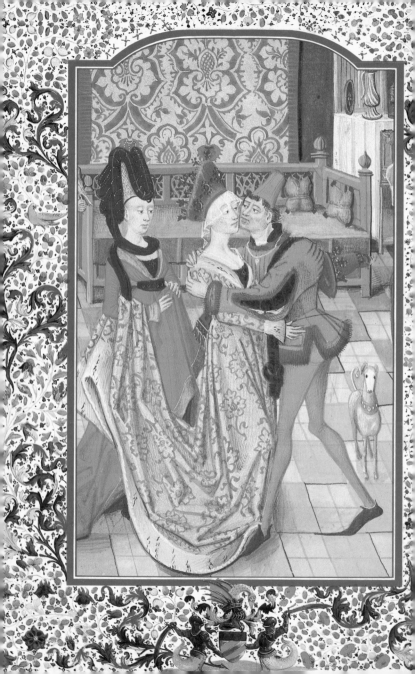

October

1

2

3

4

5

6

7

A knight bids his lady farewell

'Tehe!' quod sho, and gaif ane gawfe,
'Be still my tuchan and my calfe,
My new spanit howffing fra the sowk,
And all the blithnes of my bowk.
My sweit swanking, saif you allane,
Na leid I luiffit all this owk,
Full leif is me your graceles gane.'

Quod he, 'My claver and my curldodie,
My huny soppis, my sweit possodie,
Be not oure-bosteous to your Billie,
Be warme-hairtit and not ill-willie.
Your heilis, whit as whalis bane,
Garris riis on loft my whillylillie –
Ye brek my hart my bony ane.'

1. *gawfe*, guffaw   2. *tuchan*, stuffed calf's skin
(to encourage cow to give milk)   3. my new-
weaned little suckling lout   4. *bowk*, body
5. *swanking*, fine fellow   6. I loved no man all
this week   7. Most dear to me is your ugly
face   8. *claver*, clover; *curldodie*, plaintain
9. My honey-drink, my sheep's-head broth
10. *oure-bosteous*, over-rough   12. *heilis*, neck
13. *Garris riis*, make rise   14. *whillylillie*, penis

Scottish-English · 15th century
William Dunbar: 'In a secret place, this hindir nicht'

October

_____

8

_____

9

_____

10

_____

11

_____

12

_____

13

_____

14

_____

October

15

16

17

18

19

20

21

Fond farewells before the hunting starts in autumn

$\mathfrak{B}$lessings on the lovely lady
who does not make her lover languish;
whom the fear of the jealous one
and his punishments does not
keep from going to her knight
in the grove, the field or the orchard,
and from taking him into her chamber,
so that she may the better enjoy him,
leaving the jealous one outside the gate.
And if he speaks, may she reply:
'Say no word, make yourself scarce,
for I have my lover in my arms!'

Provencal · Late 13th century
Anonymous: Le Roman de Flamenca

October

22

23

24

25

26

27

28

They hammered the sable Panther
on to his shield as his father had borne
it before him. Over his hauberk he
wore a small white silken shift of the
Queen's (the one who was now his wife)
as it came from her naked body.
They saw no less than eighteen of them
pierced by lances and hacked through
by swords . . . She used to slip them on
again over her bare skin when her
darling returned from jousting . . .
The love of these two expressed a
deep attachment.

German · Early 13th century
Wolfram von Eschenbach: Parzival

October

29

30

31

A wife helps to show her husband's heraldic armour

November

1

2

3

4

5

6

7

Feasting after a hunting party, before the wedding

'Alas,' she said,
'whatever shall I do?
I shall never again be happy!
I loved these four knights
and desired each one
for his own sake.
There was a great deal of
good in them all
and they loved me
above everything.
Because they were so handsome,
brave, worthy and generous,
I made them compete
for my love,
not wishing to lose them all
to have just one.
I do not know which of them
to mourn the most,
but I can no longer disguise
or hide my feelings.
One of them I now see wounded
and three are dead.'

French · Late 12th century · Marie de France: Chaitivel

November

8

9

10

11

12

13

14

November

15

16

17

18

19

20

21

A young troubadour serenading his queen

Of my lady well me rejoice I may!
Her golden forehead is full narrow and small;
Her brows are like dim, red coral;
And as the jet her eyes glisten ay.

Her baggy cheeks are as soft as clay,
with large jaws and substantial.

Her nose a pentice is that never shall
Rein in her mouth though she uprightes lay.

Her mouth is nothing scant with lips gray;
Her chin unnethe may be seen at all.

Her comely body is shaped like a football,
And she sings full like a papejay.

ay, always   *pentice*, overhanging roof   *uprightes*, face
upwards   *unnethe*, scarcely   *papejay*, parrot

English · Early 15th century
Thomas Hoccleve: 'Of my lady well me rejoice I may'

November

_____

22

_____

23

_____

24

_____

25

_____

26

_____

27

_____

28

_____

Go heart, hurt with adversity,
And let my lady thy wounds see!
And tell her this, as I tell thee:
    Farewell my joy, and welcome pain,
    Until I see my lady again.

English · Late 15th–early 16th century · Anonymous

Love and Youth embracing

November

___

29

___

30

___

Keep your kiss to yourself,
white-toothed young virgin!
In your kiss I find no taste;
keep your lips away from me.

A kiss far sweeter than honey
I got from a married woman for love;
I shall not find, till Doomsday,
taste in another kiss after that.

Until I see that one herself, through the
will of the One Son of God of grace,
I shall love no woman, old nor young,
since *her* kiss is as it is.

Irish · 15th–16th century
Anonymous: 'Take Those Lips Away' tr. Kenneth Jackson

December

1

2

3

4

5

6

7

Love's playtime in a snowy landscape

Down in the valley,
leaves fall from the trees,
the branches are bare.
All the flowers have faded,
their blossom was so beautiful.
The frost attacks many herbs
and kills them. I grieve.
But if the winter is so cold,
there must be new joys.

Help me sing a joy
a hundred thousand times greater
than the buds of May.
I will sing of roses
on the red cheeks of my lady . . .
Could I win her favour,
this lovely lady would give me such joy
that I would need no other.

German · Early 14th century · Wizlaw

December

8

9

10

11

12

13

14

December

15

_____

16

_____

17

_____

18

_____

19

_____

20

_____

21

_____

The stately dance of Love and Courtesy

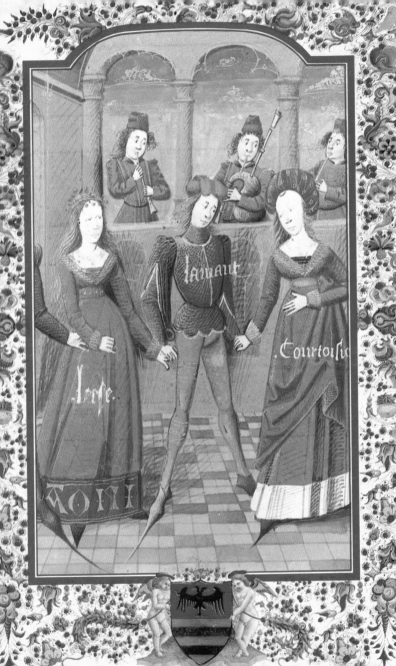

𝕬 woman who loves
may freely accept from her lover
the following:
a handkerchief, a fillet for the hair,
a wreath of gold or silver,
a breastpin, a mirror, a girdle,
a purse, a tassel, a comb,
sleeves, gloves, a ring, a compact,
a picture, a wash basin,
little dishes, trays, a flag as a souvenir,
and, to speak in general terms,
a woman may accept from her lover
any little gift which may be useful
for the care of the person
or pleasing to look at or which
may call the lover to her mind,
if it is clear that in accepting the gift
she is free from all avarice.

Latin (France) · Late 12th century
Andreas Capellanus: The Art of Courtly Love

December

22

23

24

25

26

27

28

In youth I served my time
    To kissing and love-making;
Now that I must retire
    I feel my heart is breaking.

Love's a great trade indeed;
    I have loved and cannot doubt it.
That I should live is strange
    For life's a waste without it —

And memory makes a torment
    Of all my past blisses —
Ah, God, ah God! 'tis food today
    That feeds me and not kisses.

Irish · 15th–early 16th century · Anonymous

December

29

30

31

The flower of Florentine youth, saluting his beloved

Epilogue

Love is soft and love is sweet, and speaks in accents fair;
Love is mighty agony, and love is mighty care;
Love is utmost ecstasy and love is keen to dare:
Love is wretched misery: to live with, it's despair.

Love's a lottery, mars your luck or gives you pleasures gay;
Love is lecherous, love is loose, and likely to betray;
Love's a tyrant here on earth, not easy to gainsay;
Love throughout this land of ours sends faithful ones astray.

Love's a stern and valiant knight, strong astride a steed;
Love's a thing that pleasures every longing woman's need;
Love persists and keeps its heat like any glowing gleed:
Love puts girls in floods of tears, they rage and cry indeed.

Love maintains his bailiwick in every path and street;
Love can wet with tears the cheek of any maiden sweet;
Love by chance brings misery inflamed with fever heat;
Love is wise and love is wary, wants its way complete.

Love's the softest, sweetest thing that in the heart may sleep;
Love is craft, and for its woes is well equipped to weep;
Love is false and love is eager, forces folk to long;
Love is foolish, love is firm, and love is comfort strong:
Love's a marvel to the man who treats of it in song.

Love is weal and love is woe, in gladness can maintain us;
Love is life and love is death, and love can well sustain us.

If love had strength for suffering as first it has when keen,
Then love would be the worthiest thing the world had ever seen;
But this is what is sung of it, and so it's ever been;
'Love begins in mighty pain and ends in grief and spleen,
With noble lady, steady wife, with virgin or with queen!'

English · 13th–14th century · Anonymous

Picture Credits

Dec. 1: January, from fresco cycle of the Twelve Months, Castello del Buonconsiglio, Trento (Ph: Scala)

Dec. 15: Bodleian Library, Oxford. Ms.Douce 364 fol.8r.

Dec. 29: Biblioteca Trivulziana, Milan. Ms.2167 fol.10v.

Borders

Jan.: Musée Jacquemart-André. Ms.2 fol.142v (Ph: Bulloz)

Feb.: Biblioteca Comunale, Siena (Ph: Scala)

Mar.: Biblioteca, Palacio Real, Madrid (Ph: Arxiu Mas)

Apr.: Copyright Bibliothèque Royale Albert 1er, Brussels. Ms.II060-61 fol.186

May: Bibliothèque Nationale, Paris. Ms.Fr.9087 fol.207v (Ph: Edimages)

June: *Book of the Fraternity of Our Lady's Assumption*. Skinners' Company, London

July: Bodleian Library, Oxford. Ms.Bodley 283 fol.1r.

Aug.: Bibliothèque Nationale, Paris. Ms.7853 Fr.1226 fol.7

Sept.: Bibliothèque Nationale, Paris. Ms.Fr.23279 fol.81 (Ph: Edimages)

Oct.: Bibliothèque Nationale, Paris. Ms.Fr.87 fol.117

Nov.: The Master and Fellows of Corpus Christi College, Cambridge. Ms.61 frontis./fol.1v.

Dec.: J. Bianchino, *Astrologica*. Biblioteca, Ferrara (Ph: Scala)